D0013436

Storming
Hell's Brazen Gates

Isaiah 45:2

through militant, violent,
prevailing prayer!

Dick Bernal

Unless otherwise noted, all Scripture references are taken from the New King James Version of the Bible.

Scriptures marked KJV are taken from the King James Version of the Bible.

Storming Hell's Brazen Gates
 Isaiah 45:2
ISBN 0-88144-124-4
© Copyright 1988 by Dick Bernal
175 Nortech Parkway
San Jose, CA 95134
Second Printing, March 1997

Published by Jubilee Christian Center
175 Nortech Parkway
San Jose, CA 95134

This Book is Dedicated To:

My wife, Carla ...
>one bold lady for the Lord!

Our church ...
>Thank you!

Friends
>who stick closer than a brother.

The praying pastors and believers of our cities...
>"Keep Standing!"
>and ...

To you, the reader.
>Join us as we purge the skies, Storm Hell's Brazen Gates, and take back our cities from the enemy.

Apollyon

"Destroyer"

Babylon, founded by Nimrod, was more than just a city. It was a laboratory for Satan's use in perverting the worship of God. From here the deceiver of the ages would "confound" true worship. His diversionary tactics can be traced throughout history. The Babylonian Empire rose quickly after the Flood, but met with the fate of all empires that worship false gods ... destruction!

Babylon has always been more than a city ... it is a spirit!

It is the spirit of alienation from God which has corrupted every form of human life. This spirit has set up "high places" over my city and yours. The purpose of this book is to give the reader instruction in the methods of storming hell's gates, pulling down strongholds, and purging the skies.

Will you join me in reclaiming that which the devil has stolen from us?

In May of 1982 Rev. Larry Huggins gave a word of encouragement to this new pastor and his newly-organized little church:

"As I was landing in San Jose, I saw the skies over your city as a great bowl made of brass. And the Lord showed me the holes punched through it because of the believers' efforts and prayers through the local churches - but the Lord desires to open the skies above the entire valley and allow more than just a ray or two of light to shine through.

"He wants to flood you with blessing. 'Keep teaching faith and endurance, keep praying and seeking My Face,' " the Lord said through Pastor Huggins, " 'and surely you will see this come to pass!' "

Contents

Preface

The following is a story told by Dr. Doyle "Buddy" Harrison.

Around the turn of the century there was a passageway between Manhattan and Long Island called "Hell's Gate." It had been so named because of the difficulty ships had in entering it.

Captains and crews very cautiously approached this notorious navigational hazard. In the course of time, many ships were destroyed or severely damaged, and lives were lost. In fact, there was an old sailor's adage, "Many men who were godless entered hell through that awful gate!"

As the problem continued to compound, the city fathers of New York decided to take drastic action. They brought in skilled engineers to study the area and come up with a satisfactory solution.

It was soon determined that dredging would not be enough. The only alternative was to blast away the offending channel's "gates."

The explosive charges were carefully laid. The wiring was completed. The blast-off switch was positioned in the mayor's office, for by now this had become a media event and the local population's interest and concern had been aroused.

On the appointed day the mayor's small daughter was present to witness what was about to happen. On a whim, the mayor said to her, "Honey, why don't you push the button to set off the blast?"

Please bear in mind that this little girl knew nothing about reefs or tides. She was completely ignorant of all the technical arrangements. The fact was, she barely understood what all the fuss was about.

But because her father said, "Do it, honey," she did it!

The mayor's office was in the heart of the city, far removed from the channel. Neither of them saw or heard anything after the act. But, when a few minutes had elapsed, the phone rang and a voice on the other end of the line said just five words: "Hell's Gate is no more!"

Introduction

"Don't be nervous, Bernal," I keep telling myself as I approach the pulpit of the world's largest church, Yoido Full Gospel, in Seoul, Korea. This church has an active membership of over a half-million people and is growing at the rate of 10,000 a month! When its pastor, Dr. Paul Yonggi Cho, first invited me to preach there, I was flattered beyond words. Then he told me I was scheduled for Wednesday afternoon. I must admit that I felt a little disappointed. I knew that even the most committed of Korean believers had to work like the rest of us, and I couldn't imagine that there would be many attending that service.

At last that special Wednesday afternoon arrived. As we left our hotel and started for Yoido Island, a rainstorm hit Seoul. "Great!" I thought. "Now I know the place will be practically empty." Then, when we arrived, Dr. Cho mentioned that this service was an experimental one to see how well the congregation responded to it. Oh well, thank the good Lord that Dennis Kim was with me to interpret. Dennis is a successful lawyer, a Korean member of my church in San Jose. He was in Seoul at the time on business and was also enjoying sessions of Dr. Cho's annual Church Growth Conference.

My wife Carla, Dennis Kim and I were ushered into Dr. Cho's office for prayer and fellowship before the service.

Promptly at two o'clock the singing began. We were then escorted to the platform.

To my utter astonishment, the place was packed to capacity! There were over 20,000 people filling the sanctuary, and even more had filled the overflow auditoriums, which were equipped with closed-circuit television monitors.

Here we were on a stormy Wednesday afternoon ... with circumstances which in the natural would have been disastrous ... and instead, we had a glorious time of refreshing!

My sermon topic that afternoon was "The Anointing of God." I shared about a crusade I had conducted in India a few years earlier. I noticed that every time I mentioned spiritual warfare and the casting out of demons, the congregation seemed to come alive and began to applaud. When I was through, I returned to my seat next to Dr. Cho, who leaned over and grabbed my arm. I thought he was about to exchange some nicety such as "good job," or some other compliment; but he didn't. Rather, he began prophesying in the Spirit. "Open your eyes," he said. "What do you see?" I replied, "I see 20,000 plus people in the church on a rainy Wednesday afternoon!" He continued, "You can have the same thing in your city if you will obey the voice of the Lord!"

That Word from Above shot through me like a bolt of lightning. And since that time, like a consuming fire, it has launched me on a quest which is revolutionizing my perspective - and my ministry! I know that the San Francisco Bay Area is virtually the only major population center in America that has never experienced a real Holy Ghost revival. So I began to seek answers from the Word to determine why. Not long after my return from Korea, I was spending some time with my dear friend, the late Dr. Lester

Sumrall. I knew that he was one of the first people I should talk to, for he was a veteran of over 50 years of spiritual warfare.

"Doc, why Korea?" I asked. "What is the reason for this tremendous move of God which is reshaping a whole nation, once an obscure land overshadowed by its neighbors? Why is it now coming onto the world scene like a sleeping giant?" Without a moment's hesitation, he replied, "Because they have purged the skies." He was so matter-of-fact that his response really took me by surprise. He continued, saying, "The success of their churches cannot be measured in programs, but in their militant prayers. They attacked the principality over Seoul and dethroned its prince first before they started building large churches, schools, and other projects, which, to Americans, are the main focus of ministry and church growth." As I thought about this profound premise of Dr. Sumrall, I remembered a comment made by Dr. Cho's mother-in-law a few years previously. She had said, "You Americans like to preach one hour and pray ten minutes. We Koreans like to pray one hour and preach ten minutes." At her invitation I held a two-day crusade at the world-renowned Prayer Mountain just outside of Seoul City. That experience confirmed her statement. Those people would literally rather pray than eat! Just to see thousands of believers praying with every ounce of energy, hour upon hour, was a convicting and convincing sight, to say the least. When I returned home from Korea I determined that I would re-evaluate the main focus of our church.

First, I wanted to find out who or what was perched over the Bay Area; and second, I intended to plan a strategy of attack upon its stronghold!

I began to read books on successful revivals. I talked to people like my fellow San Francisco Bay Area native,

Mario Murillo. The teachings of leaders like Jack Hayford, John Dawson, Larry Lea, C.M. Ward and others began to help me put the pieces of the puzzle together. It was often just a word or phrase that kept me on the track.

With much prayer, and a great deal of research in the Word and in published texts, I have something of great significance to share with you. I believe that the Holy Spirit has given it to me for this purpose. It will revolutionize your spiritual outlook and open new doors of understanding for you.

1

The Awakening

The apparent problem with the Church today is that its primary focus has been on the horizontal plane. Oh sure, we praise God and lift up holy hands to pray (nice, passive petitions, primarily), but in reality, most of our prayer efforts have been directed toward man. For example, we petition the city to approve of our dreams, exploit every device in the book to get new people into our churches, pass out tracts to waitresses, witness to reprobates, picket the porn shops, and so on. Yet, with all our good intentions, we are still losing the battle.

Redeeming the Time for the Days Are Evil

It is time the Church of Jesus Christ united its efforts to open the brazen skies over the cities and utterly destroy the gates of hell through militant, violent, prevailing prayer!

The skies over our planet are, for the most part, closed. What do I mean? "In the beginning God created the heavens and the earth" (Genesis 1:1). The heavens and earth were free from sin, and God's presence and blessing were unhindered. Everything was, as the Scripture says, "Good." But not for long, because Satan, in one of his many disguises, came on the scene. He didn't appear as a loathsome snake slithering up to Eve. He came as a beautiful and desirable creature, apparently the most gorgeous of the animal creation. You know the story; the tempter's scheme prevailed and man was, for the first time, bound by sin.

Because of this, the very nature of Satan (pride and rebellion) was lodged deep in the heart of man - and so it is until this day!

As each generation passes, the power of sin increases. The heavenlies, once clear and yielding, are now infested by an arrogant prince of darkness. His high-ranking principalities are feverishly occupied with setting up blockades to separate man from his Creator.

The Brass Blockade

God knows that the only way to keep a channel open between heaven and earth is through a covenant. So He finds willing men, such as Abram (Abraham), who will work with Him to keep the earth from being totally closed out. God's covenant, or holy contract, links man to his Creator in a spiritually, as well as legally, binding agreement.

God laid down the law through Moses. In Deuteronomy 28, He lists the blessings for obedience to this law and the curses for disobedience.

He says, "If you diligently obey the voice of the Lord your God, to observe carefully all His commandments which I command you today, the Lord your God will set you on high above all the nations of the earth."

He continues by saying, "The Lord will open to you His good treasure, the heavens, to give rain to your land in its season, and to bless all the work of your hand. You shall lend to many nations and you shall not borrow." Please notice that it says, "If you obey, I will open the heavens."

Now let's take a look at the curses He promises in verse 23: "Your heavens which are over your head shall be bronze, and the earth which is under you shall be iron. The Lord will change the rain of your land to powder and dust;

from the heaven it shall come down on you until you are destroyed." This was to be the fruit for disobedience to God's statutes and commandments.

Bronze or brass is used in many places in the Bible as a type of sin. For instance, the brazen altar, the brazen serpent, and the Grecian Empire represented by brass in Daniel chapter 2 all speak of sin. Brass, an alloy comprised of copper, zinc and small amounts of other metals, looks like gold from a distance. But closer scrutiny reveals its true character - something that looks like gold but isn't. We can safely say that whenever man walks contrary to God's ways, the skies above him, his home, city, and even nation are skies of brass shutting out heaven's blessings.

The Master Opener

This helps us to understand the Scripture found in John 1:48-51. Here Nathanael was shocked when Jesus told him that in a vision He had observed him under a fig tree even before Philip had summoned him. Totally flabbergasted, Nathanael replied, "... You are the Son of God! You are the King of Israel!" Jesus replied, "Because I said to you, 'I saw you under the fig tree,' do you believe? You will see greater things than these ... Most assuredly I say to you, hereafter you shall see heaven open, and the angels of God ascending and descending upon the Son of Man."

When Jesus says, "You will see the heavens open," we may come to the obvious conclusion that they must be closed.

What is it that closes heaven? Satan? No, Satan and his host feed on man's sin. They have no power or authority outside of that which man abdicates through disobedience. Jesus, the Perfect One, says, "Every place I go, every town, village, home, everywhere I set My foot, you will see the skies over Me part and angels [ministering servants] slip through and assist Me in My work."

In Nathanael's day, as today, the skies over Israel were closed. They were skies of brass. Israel had become religious instead of righteous. The Holy Temple itself had become a booming money-maker for the priests. Israel hadn't had a prophet since Malachi. A heathen, cultish empire was ruling the Promised Land from Rome.

Yet Jesus, walking the land as the Son of Man (the title He Himself used more than any other), came to show all of us how we too could open the skies and allow righteousness to rain down upon us. It is essential to note His reference to the angelic helpers who are, we are told, sent to assist us in ministry.

A consecrated life of prayer, faith and action will open the heavens to us, and a life of sin will keep them closed. This is a simple truth with profound implications.

With these truths established, we are ready to attack the demonized skies over our cities (in my case, San Jose and its environs) and to blow holes in the brass of the heavenlies.

United Effort

I believe that this is what happened on the day of Pentecost: One hundred twenty prayer warriors, totally focused and in perfect harmony, blew open a hole so big that when the Spirit of God rushed through, the force of it sounded like a tornado!

Jesus said, "Before a king goes to war, he first counts the cost." In other words, he takes a survey, does a little reconnaissance. He asks, "Who am I up against? Where are the strongholds?" Jesus also warned that "before you can take the spoils, you must first bind the strongman." There are some interesting schools of thought concerning that verse, but the truth of the matter is that until we locate, identify and pull down the principalities over our cities, the spoils (the people) will remain slaves in Satan's dark kingdom. In Revelation chapter 2, our Lord instructs John to write a letter to the church at Pergamos, saying, "I know your works, and where you dwell, where Satan's throne is..." The Lord geographically pinpoints the actual seat of Satan!

Because of the intense satanic worship at Pergamos, Satan had set up shop there. I am convinced that he is no longer over Pergamos, because he moves from place to place. He goes where he can exercise the most influence.

The Ancient Enemy

I call your attention to the fact that Satan is not omnipresent. He cannot be everywhere at one time. And so he must dispatch chief rulers (principalities) to guard and protect his perverted scheme for empires, nations, provinces, states, and even cities. His diabolic driving force is aimed at keeping God's prophetic Word from being manifested. Satan still refuses to believe that his fate is sealed. As "god of this world," he will fight until the end to maintain his control of the skies.

Back in the days of Daniel we are given an illustration of a battle waged above ancient Persia. In Daniel 10:12-13, we read: "Then he said to me, 'Do not fear, Daniel, for from the first day that you set your heart to understand, and to humble yourself before your God, your words were heard; and I have come because of your words. But the prince of the kingdom of Persia withstood me twenty-one days; and behold, Michael, one of the chief princes, came to help me, for I had been left alone there with the kings of Persia.' "

2

The Great Impostor ... No More!

We are now approaching a vital phase of this teaching.

In sizing up the enemy troops, it is paramount that we understand who we are facing - a PRINCE. This is an ancient, wise, and certainly a cunning prince who has had millenniums of experience at keeping mankind from God.

The word "prince" in the Greek is *ARCHON*. From the root, *ARCHO*, meaning "to be first (in political rank or power)," *ARCHON* means "a ruler or magistrate."

Satan is a religious and political personality. Unfortunately, we the Church have often been thoroughly duped by his diversionary tactics. For the most part, we have been looking for him in the drug-infested ghettos, the homosexual districts, saloons, gambling halls, porn shops and the like. In reality, these are merely the sad manifestations of man's depravity, his base nature run amok! For such as these, you will find demons of a much lower rank in control.

However, to find the evil generals of the skies, the higher echelon of Satan's realm, you must look to the areas of real control and power - be it political, religious or economic. Wherever there is an institution that controls the lives and thoughts of the masses, this is where you will find a principality controlling conversations, desires, direction and intent, exactly as Paul described it in Ephesians 2:1-3, "And you hath he quickened, who were dead in trespasses and sins; wherein in time past ye walked according to the course of this world, according to the prince of the power of the air, the spirit that now worketh in the children of disobedience; Among whom also we all had our conversation in times past in the lusts of our flesh, fulfilling the desires of the flesh and of the mind; and were by nature the children of wrath, even as others" (KJV).

Look in the Right Places

Be assured that the prince of the power of the air does not spend his time and efforts on opening pornographic bookstores on every corner; he doesn't have to. Carnal, fleshly man will see to it that his warped desires are fulfilled.

Where Satan does spend his time and effort is in fostering new antichrist governments and churches that have an appearance of godliness, yet whose perverted doctrines deny the power thereof.

He can also be found in financial or educational systems which are designed to keep money, power, and the young from Jesus and His Church.

Failing to understand this, the Church still wants to spend its time, money and effort picketing, marching, shouting down the scoffers and feeling righteously justified after a hard day of pounding the pavement for Jesus, trying to defend God! Don't misunderstand me; I'm not against some good old-fashioned activism, but what I'm trying to emphasize is that history is proving that we are losing the war with those means! When a Holy Spirit revival hits, you won't have to exert pressure on a bookstore owner to get rid of the "girlie" magazines. He will willingly take his stand for God along with the pusher, hooker, agnostic, you name it. As one preacher put it, "Morality will never come through legislation, only through regeneration."

A few years ago I had a brainstorm. (Have you ever wondered why it's called a storm?) San Jose has one of the nation's larger flea markets. Thousands of people converge upon it each weekend. I reasoned, "Why not set up a booth there for counseling, preaching and passing out tracts?"

My problems began when some of my over-zealous parishioners began to engage in shouting matches with passersby. Some of these were rough-looking types with tattoos and motorcycle jackets, good ol' boys who had had more than their share of brew.

Some of the men helping me were from pretty rough backgrounds themselves. They were ex-cons, former junkies and former gang leaders who had found Christ in prison.

They thought it was OK to get entangled in arguments with the shoppers. It became so heated one Saturday that I thought the police would arrive and arrest everyone, including me!

"Guys," I said, "this is not the reason we are here. Would Jesus condemn these poor lost souls in such a manner?" I opened my Bible to Proverbs 9:7-8 and read, "He who reproves a scoffer gets shame for himself, And he who rebukes a wicked man gets himself a blemish. Do not reprove a scoffer lest he hate you ..."

The reason that some folks resist the Gospel is not because of God or Christ. Most people have no problem with the Lord. They even have a certain respect for "The Man Upstairs," but the reason they don't come to church is because of "church people"!

In thirty-two years I found very few church people that I liked. I thought them judgmental, hard, and self-righteous - and those were some of their better traits!

No, Jesus didn't keep me out of His Church. I was afraid that if I went, I'd become like the ones I had met. Thank God, all that's changing. We are learning that we can catch more fish with enticing bait than we can with stones. Children throw rocks. Skilled anglers gently lay a delicious looking hook close to the target's mouth.

Paul said, "... Thus I fight: not as one who beats the air" (II Corinthians 9:26). Satan doesn't mind our putting up a fight as long as our efforts are as futile as one who "beats the air." It's when our blows begin to land on his strategic areas of influence that he takes nervous notice.

As a seasoned fisherman, I have enough sense to change "plugs" after several attempts bring no bites. A boxer will tell you that it doesn't always take a volley of punches to bring an opponent down ... just one, directed at his most vulnerable spot!

As a friend of mine says, "Let's work smarter ... not harder."

3
Search and Destroy

The next question with which we shall be dealing is, "How do we identify the ARCHE (principality or principalities) over our cities?" At a conference which I recently attended in Southern California, a young minister said, "We first have to look at who and what kind of people settled in our area before we can determine what kind of spirit now dominates the community."

In our case, here in the San Francisco Bay Area (and Central California), we have to examine our roots and our origins. Historians agree that modern California was born with the discovery of gold at Sutter's Mill, near what is now Sacramento, around the year 1850.

This momentous event gave an immediate tilt to the United States. Need I describe the type of individual that headed for California? Every fortune-seeking, greedy, nomadic adventurer dropped everything and abandoned family, friends and home, blindly seeking the pot of gold that he fancied lay at the end of the California rainbow.

It's no surprise that San Francisco quickly became the Barbary Coast. An article which I recently read said that California has become a laboratory for new modes of living because of the steady streams of people who are attracted here. No wonder we have such a liberal political scene today. The hippie movement and the so-called sexual revolution claim the Bay Area as their launching pads.

One of the New Age Movement's recent publications calls Santa Clara County its headquarters. Where else in our nation could a Silicon Valley spring up virtually overnight? These are the new forty-niners, gambling this time with computer chips instead of poker chips. It has been said that San Francisco invents it, Los Angeles perfects it, and New York markets it and sends it to Europe!

Its Name Is "Self"

It is obvious to me that the ruling entity over the Bay Area is a selfish, greedy, nomadic type who was invited here over 140 years ago by our predecessors, the pioneers. In prayer, the Holy Spirit impressed upon me that the tide of the ruling principality over our area is "SELF."

Lesser rulers include "perversion," "murder," "addiction," "greed," "suicide," and "contention," just to name a few of those inhabiting the skies from Carmel to Marin County (just north of San Francisco). Spiritually speaking, a person who is "tuned in" can drive from one community to the next and sense the change in spiritual activity. For example, San Francisco is only across the Bay from Oakland, yet these two are contrasting cities. They have a different "feel" ... even to a person who is not spiritually sensitive. Why? Ruling spirits! In San Francisco the spirit of perversion prevails, while in Oakland the spirit is murder and addiction.

Santa Cruz, a beautiful little hamlet twenty-five miles from San Jose, has a spirit of death over it. Santa Cruz has become an important occult center in America. Recently it was called the "capital of the serial killers." Just a half-hour away in Silicon Valley one must battle the spirit of greed. Satan's principalities are very competitive and territorial. In researching this book I visited a famous and strategic landmark right here in San Jose, the Rosicrucians' Egyptian Museum. The Rosicrucians, or AMORC (Ancient Mystic Order Rosae Crucis), are members of a secret society which researches ancient religions. They claim that they are a non-religious organization, yet their bookstore is full of heresies denouncing the work of the cross as a fake plot conceived by our Lord Himself. They also exalt Lucifer as a force of enlightenment. Their free brochures speak of the quest for "Self"!

They teach that being linked with the cosmic forces which flow through us is the ultimate. Their buzz words have a taint of New Age-ism: aura, psychic energy, vibrations, creativity, mastering of life, infinite consciousness, and so on. Their brochures boast of a new openness and awareness unrestricted by regimentation. They claim that "For centuries men and women have been aided in penetrating the unrevealed attributes of 'Self.' " They present "subjects, ideas and useful experiments which are challenging." I can imagine ...

Now, let's return to our previous thoughts on area heritage.

Settlers Settled Down

It is interesting to compare the West Coast founding fathers with those who settled in the Midwest, the Bible Belt. For the most part, those who settled in the Midwest were farmers, ranchers, people of substance, family oriented, hard-working and deeply religious. This explains why their churches are larger, more numerous and better attended than those in our area. Their skies are more open because they have been bombarded with prayer for generations and Satan's seats of authority have truly been weakened.

I am just beginning to understand why it is so difficult

to keep folks in church, on the job, married, and in school around here. People seem to be so fragmented, restless, uneasy and frustrated without an obvious reason. The "why?" is answered this way - because the ruling prince is seeing to it! Like a giant puppeteer, he is continually pulling their strings.

4

The Ancient Deities

My research is leading me deeper into the whys and wherefores of the ruling principalities of this particular place: the San Francisco Bay Area. On a recent factfinding mission, one of our members was at the State Capitol in Sacramento. He was looking around the building and came upon a giant replica of the State Seal of California. Inasmuch as I had been teaching on the demonic influences over California, he was particularly astonished to find that the predominant figure on the seal was that of a Roman goddess (a demon principality) named Minerva!

Some scholars believe that the Roman cult of Minerva was the same as that of Athena in the Grecian culture. Minerva (Athena) is one of the Olympians supposed to have been born out of the head of Zeus. He was the most powerful of all the ancient Greek and Roman gods, ruler of heaven and earth, and prince over all other gods and men. It is interesting to note that Milton uses this myth to describe the birth of sin out of the head of Satan *(Paradise Lost,* ii, 752-758).

As the goddess of wisdom, commerce, the arts, professions, schools and war, Minerva was the protectress over cities. The worship of Minerva attained its greatest following during the time of the Etruscan kings.

Who Is She?

According to tradition, the cult of Minerva originated around 241 BC in Falerri, even though a temple had already been dedicated to her in Rome prior to that date.

Minerva, the protectress of the cities, was to see that all she represented became reality. She was a dominant presence in early Rome, which of course became everything she represents.

The point that we need to emphasize is that those cities where the worship of these "deities" was predominant have either been destroyed or are presently mere shadows of their former greatness (e.g., Athens, Rome, Ephesus).

You ask, "What is the connection?" Well, it's obvious that these ruling spirits are out to destroy man one way or another. Believe it; war, greed, perversion, human sacrifice, disease and any other vile device they can conjure up is at their disposal.

Firsthand Experience

Having personally ministered in India, I can tell you as an eye witness that their poverty and disease is not from lack of raw materials or arable land. Their curse stems from false worship of demon gods! They starve while worshipping a cow, the very same animal that gives us our juicy steaks and tasty barbecues.

During a crusade I held in India, I personally encountered several different kinds of demons. There were sniveling, weak, timid ones who fled at the first sign of resistance. Then there were the arrogant, stubborn ones who sneered and boasted of their strength and power.

The first night I preached in an open-air meeting and I called for the sick to come forward for prayer. As I recall, I asked for all who were having respiratory problems. To my amazement, hundreds came. My first reaction was, "My Lord, how can I effectively pray for such a great multitude?" It was already midnight. Besides that, I was personally exhausted from jet lag and lack of sleep.

Personal comforts aside, we began to line up those who were seeking healing into some sort of order so that they could pass by and be prayed for.

If Looks Could Kill!

The second person to pass by was a pleasant-looking young Hindu woman around 18 years of age. As I touched her, she fell at my feet and actually began slithering like a snake. As you know, many Hindus worship snakes. Her eyes bulged and her tongue darted in and out at a supernatural speed. She really took on the appearance of a serpent. Talk about getting a crash course in demonology - this was it!

"Demons, Pastor Dick, demons!" cried the Indian ministers who were assisting me. I answered, "Yeah, I know what it is, but I sure haven't seen the likes of this in San Jose!" Even though my skin was literally crawling and the hair on my head was standing on end, I knew that I hadn't come 13,000 miles to be intimidated by some snake demon! Bless God, the Name of Jesus still packs the same punch that it did over 1,900 years ago, and I can report that the evil presence was cast out with a single command.

For the next seven days I saw every manifestation imaginable. I was cursed, spit at, mocked, and screamed at by strange voices coming out of otherwise normal-looking people.

The Strong Ones

One woman who was about 25 years old followed us from town to town. Right at the time the altar call was being given she would throw a fit, thus drawing attention to herself and disrupting the invitation. I took her aside one night and began ministering the Name of Jesus. Her eyes rolled back in her head, she laughed, she screamed, she passed out. It seemed that the harder I tried to set her free, the uglier she got. I was a little confused because my efforts seemed so futile. Yet otherwise we were having great results with the masses.

Later I discovered that this woman was inviting all the demons that we were casting out of the others into herself. Jesus said in Matthew 17:21, "However, this kind does not go out except by prayer and fasting." In my exhausted state, I was not fresh with the Spirit that comes during prayer and fasting. I was apparently leaning too much on the arm of the flesh. That evening I fell deathly ill. A tremendous fever seized me and I had a bad case of chills. This witch had put a curse on me and I began to think I was dying. Fear tried to grip me, but thanks be to God, His Spirit rose up within me. I prayed in the Spirit at the top of my lungs for hours.

The next morning, which was Sunday, I was invited to speak at a Lutheran Church about forty miles from where I was staying. I must have looked like death warmed over, but I went anyway and gave them my best shot.

Every ten or fifteen minutes I would say, "Please excuse me," as I headed for the restroom. When I returned, those sweet folks would just grin and we'd take up where we left off.

Shake It Off!

After my return to the States it took me at least six months to pray off the effects of that curse. In those days I was young in the ministry, extremely green and idealistic, to say the least. But here I'd like to say that God's mercy and grace covers our lack of experience or we'd all be easy prey for demons!

Back to Minerva

Getting back to Minerva, the forms of worship directed toward her were magic, divination, incantations, sacrifices (both blood and bloodless), prayers, and ritualistic dancing. According to legend, Minerva was brash, arrogant and strong-willed. Her name comes from the root *manas or mens*. She was dressed like a man and had decidedly masculine characteristics. As for war, her reputation rivaled that of Mars, the god of war.

Consider this: The great seal of California, the stamp of state authority and approval, is a demon spirit! Though she is disguised as a mythological Roman goddess overlooking San Francisco Bay, she is actually a demon spirit. Have no doubt of that!

I was told by a pastor who ministers in San Francisco, "My greatest challenge is making men out of wimps and ladies out of brassy women." Isn't it curious that San Francisco, the Silicon Valley and even the state of California have become everything that Minerva represents? In Silicon Valley, wisdom - Stanford and Cal Berkeley are called the mind of America. And the arts - Hollywood and Los Angeles are the media centers of the world. As for commerce, if California were a separate country, our GNP (Gross National Product) would rank #6 in the world. Minerva represents war; and most of the technology and instrumentation in nuclear weaponry is developed right here. Star Wars and laser technology are being primarily researched less than 20 miles from our church. Before the military downsizing of the Clinton administration California boasted some of the largest aircraft plants and shipyards in the nation.

The spirit of Minerva is alive!

He Saw Them!

In Howard Pittman's book, *Demons, An Eyewitness Account* he describes an out-of-body experience he had when he suffered an apparently fatal rupture of an internal artery. As doctors frantically endeavored to save his life, he left his body and his spirit was escorted by an angel of the Lord into the second heaven (the heavenlies). This angel showed Pittman the five ranks of evil spirits who will be the most prominent in the end times. The chief rulers under Satan were called "warring spirits." He observed one particular spirit who was very tall. He was an athletic type, quite striking really, and dressed in a Roman soldier's uniform. (Remember Minerva on the State Seal of California?)

Those creatures that he was shown were stunning to behold, but they were obviously full of hate and pride. They displayed their contempt for the lower ranking spirits as well.

It is interesting to note a remarkable similarity to the Hindu caste system - from the Brahmans down to the untouchables. In a nation so given over to idolatry, it is little wonder that there are so many parallels to the system of their controllers in the heavenlies.

Mr. Pittman continues by describing the descending order of spirits. From the rulers of darkness and spiritual hosts of wickedness in heavenly places, the list continues down to the lowliest of minions. We can find confirmation of this in Ephesians 6:12, "For we do not wrestle against flesh and blood, but against principalities, against powers, against the rulers of the darkness of this age, against spiritual hosts of wickedness in the heavenly places."

The mission of these spirits, according to rank, was to induce greed, hunger for power, false doctrines (this also pertains to some so-called Christian circles), infirmities, diseases, mental torment, possession, addictions, and so on.

The personal appearance of each demon was different. For instance, the spirit of greed looked very much like today's businessman. He looked "together," pleasant and personable. Yet behind the facade he was full of cunning, deception and perversion, controlling the finances of the world!

Mr. Pittman's description of the religious spirit was fascinating. This particular one was half man and half beast - which comes as no surprise, does it? We know that the origin of pagan religion and idolatry can be traced back to Cush and his son, Nimrod, the founder and builder of Babylon and the tower of Babel.

Quoting Gwen Shaw's excellent book, *Redeeming the Land* (pp. 41-42), "Nimrod the Centaur: The fabulous half-horse, half-man who is prevalent in Greek mythology is believed to commemorate the original man who taught the world horsemanship. But he did not originate in Greece. The Greeks got the Centaur from Babylon. Ancient coins depicting the Centaur prove this. The Centaur, like the warrior Orion, is found in the Zodiac. The Greeks acknowledge that the original Centaur was the same as Kronos and Saturn. Saturn was the father of the gods (i.e., Nimrod) who is always depicted on the ancient coins with a bow - but no arrows. He became the conqueror of the souls of men."

Is there any connection between him and the rider on the white horse in Revelation 6:2? "And I looked and behold, a white horse. And he who sat on it had a bow..."

You see, he also has a bow and no arrows. Could the rider of Revelation be another godless "Nimrod" who will come forth as a mighty and powerful apostate leader of false religion, hunting and conquering the souls of men?

The huntsman Centaur can be traced to all nations, even to India.

I believe it is important, once again, to note that Satan is not anti-religion, he is *antichrist!* He himself craves worship. This means that he is not about to eliminate "religion," but rather he creates diversions away from the true and living God. How? By starting "new" religious ways which seemingly lead to God, but which, in reality, lead to the seat of the prince of darkness, Satan himself!

The Unholy Trinity

Gwen Shaw also traces the very roots of false worship to the original "unholy trinity" in her book. This evil group is comprised of Cush, whose father Ham ignited a curse from Noah's father (Genesis 9:18-27); Nimrod his son, and Semiramis, Nimrod's wife. These three were eventually exalted and worshipped as gods.

After Nimrod's death, Semiramis convinced the gullible world that she was actually Nimrod's mother. She also claimed that her new son (probably conceived out of wedlock by another) was the risen liberator of the curse of Genesis 9:24-27.

You see, the ancient world was well aware of Genesis 3:15, "And I will put enmity between ... your seed and her Seed; He shall bruise your head and you shall bruise His heel."

Nearly every culture has a hero slaying the old serpent. And Semiramis was to be the first. Her son, through an immaculate conception (another fabricated lie) was indeed Nimrod's second coming. "He will lift the curse," she proclaims!

Well, the sly old devil has his counterfeit father, Cush; the son, Nimrod; and the holy mother, Semiramis.

Listen to the word that the Lord spoke against Babylon and against the land of the Chaldeans by Jeremiah the prophet. "Declare among the nations, Proclaim, and set up a standard; Proclaim, and do not conceal it - Say, 'Babylon is taken, Bel is shamed. Merodach is broken in pieces; Her idols are humiliated, Her images are broken in pieces'" (Jeremiah 50:2). The chief of Babylon was called *MARDUK* (or in the Hebrew, *Merodach).* Scholars have connected him to Nimrod. In the Aramaic language of later Babylonia, Marduk was usually called Bel (Lord). To the Israelite captives who were brought to Babylon by Nebuchadnezzar in 597 and 587 BC, Bel's religion was strange and hateful. His original temple tower, or *ziggurat* where Hammurabi had worshipped, is thought by some to have been the biblical Tower of Babel. The prophet Jeremiah pronounced doom on the god as well as on the state: "Babylon is taken, Bel is confounded, Merodach [Marduk] is broken in pieces... " (Jeremiah 50:2, KJV)

"According to the Apocrypha, Daniel destroyed Bel's temple and converted the Babylonian king (Daniel 14 in the Douay Bible). Cyrus, the Persian Empire builder, acknowledged Marduk's influence when he captured Babylon in 539 BC, claiming that the god had personally chosen him to rule. In 331, when Alexander the Great took the city, he gave orders to rebuild Marduk's ancient ziggurat but died before the work could be begun." (W.F. Albright, *From Stone Age to Christianity.)* Throughout history, many generations have worshipped a "holy mother and divine child." Even the modern-day worship of Mary can be traced back to this perverted plot of Semiramis.

Female deities have, for centuries, dominated the religious scene, e.g. Diana, Athena, and India's Kali, to name just a few of the notables. I am convinced that these strong female entities are the spirits behind homosexuality. What else could drive a man to dress, talk and wear makeup like a woman, and to desire sex with another man?

It would behoove us to look at the Pelasgian (early Greek) creation myth and compare it with Scripture:

In the beginning, Eurynome, the Goddess of All Things, rose naked from Chaos, but found nothing substantial for her feet to rest upon, and therefore divided the sea from the sky, dancing lonely upon its waves. She danced toward the south, and the wind set in motion behind her seemed something new and apart with which to begin a work of creation. Wheeling about, she caught hold of this north wind, rubbed it between her hands, and behold! The great serpent Ophion. Eurynome danced to warm herself, wildly and more wildly, until Ophion, grown lustful, coiled about those divine limbs and was moved to couple with her. Now, the North Wind, who is also called Boreas, fertilizes; which is why mares often turn their hindquarters to the wind and breed foals without aid of a stallion (according to myth). So Eurynome was likewise got with child.

Next, she assumed the form of a dove, brooding on the waves and, in due process of time, laid the Universal Egg. At her bidding, Ophion coiled seven times about this egg, until it hatched and split in two. Out tumbled all things that exist, her children: sun, moon, planets, stars, the earth with its mountains and rivers, its trees, herbs, and living creatures.

Eurynome and Ophion made their home upon Mount Olympus, where he vexed her by claiming to be the author of the Universe. Forthwith she bruised his head with her heel, kicked out his teeth, and banished him to the dark caves below the earth. (*Greek Myths:* I by Robert Graves, p. 27.)

There were other versions of creation to confuse early

man. Homeric, Orphic, Olympian, the two philosophical creation myths, and the five ages of man myth were all satanically-inspired concepts of earth's origin.

The popular phrases "Mother Nature" and "Mother Earth" stem from this ancient form of "Mother Goddess" worship.

In the Pelasgian religious system, women were the dominant sex, exalted and worshipped. Man was her frightened victim. Fatherhood was not honored and conception was attributed to the wind, the eating of beans, or the accidental swallowing of an insect. Seriously! Inheritance was matrilineal and snakes were regarded as incarnations of the devil.

Satan certainly has a wild imagination! The father of all lies is a master of his trade.

One of the most exciting, as well as the most mysterious, of the divinities of the Near East is without doubt the great goddess of fruitfulness and motherhood. She has many names and many faces. The Sumerians chose to call her Inanna. Among the Semitic Assyrians and Babylonians she was called Ishtar, and among the Phoenicians, Anat. There are scores of other names besides. There are also parallel goddesses - basically a series of variations of the one archetype. Their essential features are everywhere the same, even though the emphasis varies from one people to another. For example, the Babylonians, as distinct from the Sumerians and Phoenicians, stressed the character of Ishtar as light. They linked her with the planet Venus. Ishtar is the sister of Shamash, the sun, and both are children of Sin, the moon. Akkadian prayers to Ishtar emphasize her luminous light-bearing qualities: "Thou art the light of heaven and earth, the warlike daughter of Sin ... Shining torch of heaven and earth, radiance of every dwelling place

... Torch of heaven and earth, radiance of the boundaries of the world..."

At the same time Ishtar's heroic deeds are praised. Like the Indian Devil (goddess), she is warlike; her rage is fearful; she rules by force over men and gods; she wades knee-deep in blood and is celebrated as a fearless fighter, a victorious heroine. But above all she is connected with the sexual life and reproduction of man and beast. She is the patroness of motherhood and marriage. She is the source of well-being and contentment. She herself undergoes all the phases of a woman's life. Her beloved - Dumuzi to the Sumerians, Tammuz to the Semitic Mesopotamians, Baal to the Phoenicians - appears as the archetype of the bridegroom, or the young husband. Of course, Inanna/Ishtar is depicted as inconstant. It is said that she is faithless and lets her lover die. And when he dies the whole world mourns. This is the time when the waters fail and vegetation dries up. Cruelly, she lets her lover sink into the underworld. Afterwards, however, she laments and weeps over his destruction.

According to another myth, Inanna/Ishtar herself descends into the underworld, but when she reaches it, all reproduction ceases on earth. She is said to practice intercourse with other men besides Tammuz, and even with animals. Kings are flattered to be called favorites of Ishtar. Nevertheless, like Anat, her Phoenician counterpart, she remains eternally virgin.

Thus the Great Goddess of love and motherhood is a figure of many levels, dominating the whole background. She is so various and beloved that all the goddesses of the Mesopotamian and Syrian pantheon are combined in her. In the Akkadian, language, her name, Ishtar, becomes an ordinary noun meaning "godhead." She is the essence of the divine in its feminine aspect, "the essence of the feminine altogether." ("The Gods of the Near East," from *The Unknown God* by Istv'an R'acz.)

In man's passionate straining to seek his god, he feels compelled to give artistic expression through creating idols, statues, graven images and other art forms. This longing for God is deeply rooted within man. The Bible says, "God is Spirit, and those who worship Him must worship in spirit and truth" (John 4:24).

The first commandment of the ten that God delivered to Moses on Mount Sinai was, "You shall have no other gods before Me" (Exodus 20:3). The Jews of old also received this specific warning in Leviticus 26:1: "You shall not make idols for yourselves; neither a carved image nor a sacred pillar shall you rear up for yourselves; nor shall you set up an engraved stone in your land, to bow down to it; for I am the Lord your God."

In Athens, Paul's spirit was provoked within him when he saw that the city was given over to idols" (Acts 17:16). His anger seemingly turned to compassion, for he stood in the Areopagus and said, " ... Men of Athens, I perceive that in all things you are very religious; for as I was passing through and considering the objects of your worship, I even found an altar with this inscription: TO THE UNKNOWN GOD. Therefore, the One whom you worship without knowing, Him I proclaim to you: God, who made the world and everything in it, since He is Lord of heaven and earth, does not dwell in temples made with hands" (Acts 17:22-24).

Even though Paul felt a pang of sorrow for idol worshipers, he sternly warned the world in Romans 1:18-25, "For the wrath of God is revealed [not hidden] from heaven against all ungodliness and unrighteousness of men, who suppress the truth in unrighteousness, because what may be known of God is manifest in them, for God has shown it to them. For since the creation of the world His invisible attributes are clearly seen, being understood by the things that are made, even His eternal power and Godhead, so that they are without excuse, because, although they knew God, they did not glorify Him as God, nor were thankful, but became futile in their thoughts, and their foolish hearts were darkened. Professing to be wise, they became fools, and changed the glory of the incorruptible God into an image made like corruptible man - and birds and four-footed beasts and creeping things. Therefore God also gave them up to uncleaness, in the lusts of their hearts, to dishonor their bodies among themselves, who exchanged the truth of God for the lie, and worshipped and served the creature rather than the Creator, who is blessed forever. Amen."

As Walter Nigg said in the foreword of his book, *The Unknown God,* "The step from the image of God to a relationship with God is a considerable one." These idols came in various shapes and sizes, some primitively fashioned and some marvelously creative works of art.

We Americans would never think of erecting images contrary to God's Word ... would we?

If I were to ask you what America's most recognizable symbol is, you would unhesitatingly answer, "The Statue of Liberty." Before you brand me as a non-patriot, listen to a few facts: The reason for giving the statue was political. France at that time (the 1880's) was very unstable. A group of French politicians came up with a great propaganda scheme aimed at influencing the structure of the nation. The leader of this plan was Edouard-Rene' LeFebure de Laboulage. He reasoned that a great way to express criticism of their existing form of government would be to gift America with a great statue proclaiming liberty.

He explained, "Let's have the Americans position this colossal monument towards Europe, proclaiming freedom and liberty American-style for France to see." These crafty statesmen engaged the skills of Frederic Auguste Bertholdi, a great sculptor of that day.

Thirty years prior to this commission, Bertholdi had gone to Egypt to study the existing colossi of ancient times. He had a fascination for the Zeus of Phidas, the chryselephantine Athena, Diana, and the grandest of them all, the Colossus of Rhodes.

While in Egypt he was very impressed with the colossi at Thebes. Our Statue of Liberty was originally called "Liberty Enlightening the World." Our "Liberty Lady" has a striking similarity to the goddesses of old. I'm all for freedom and liberty, and for everything we're told she represents, but I'm finding my freedom and liberty in God's Word!

America is inundated with figures and symbols out of pagan pasts, but we, like Josiah before his awakening, have grown accustomed to and accepted them. They dot our landscapes like old friends.

Storming Hell's Brazen Gates

BABYLON FALLEN

For her sins have reached unto heaven, and God hath remembered her iniquities.
. . . (Revelation 18: 5)

THE CONFUSION OF TONGUES

And they said, Go to, let us build us a city and a tower, whose top may reach
unto heaven . . . So the Lord scattered them abroad from thence upon the face of all
the earth . . . (Genesis 11: 4,8)

ATHENA
From the west pediment of the so-called Temple of Aphaea at Aegina, c510 B.C. *Munich*

Olympus

The Greeks, unlike the Egyptians, made
their gods in their own image

HEAD OF APOLLO
From the west pediment of the Temple of
Zeus at Olympia, 470–456 B.C. *Olympia*

APOLLO
Red-figured Greek psykter, Pan Painter, c490
B.C. *Munich*

5

Clever Disguises

For Roman religions and Greek mythology to come face to face with Christianity is nothing new! The Apostle Paul in the Book of Acts had more than one run-in over this matter. In Acts 14:11, after Paul has healed a crippled man in Lystra, the people begin to shout, "The gods have come down to us in the likeness of men!" They proceed to call Barnabas, Zeus; and Paul, Mercury or Hermes.

In Acts 16, when Paul casts a demon out of a girl, the Bible calls the spirit "a spirit of Apollo or Python." According to legend, a huge serpent who lived on Mt. Parnassus was famous for his powers in predicting the future. Apollo supposedly killed the serpent and assumed his skills, becoming Apollo Pythias.

A female worshiper of Apollo Pythias was called a Pythoness and through her came occult messages. In other words, this girl whom Paul delivered had been possessed by a demon camouflaging himself as a famous mythological hero. Paul demonstrated how helpless even the strong demons are to the Name of Jesus!

In Acts 17, Paul preaches in Athens (which name comes from "Athena") on Mars Hill. What really fascinates me is Paul's ministry in Ephesus. Ephesus was a major religious center to the known world at that time. This was because of Diana, the Roman goddess of the hunt and the moon. Worship of Diana was worldwide. It is interesting to note that Ephesus was apparently a center of demonic activity. Acts 19:12 explains that many were delivered from evil spirits there. Also in Acts 19 we read the story of the sons of Sceva, a group of amateur exorcists playing church who almost lost their lives in the process. Demonic possession seemed almost the norm in Ephesus.

It was also in Ephesus that multitudes brought books to Paul to be burned; books on the occult, magic, astrology, seances, curse-placing and other black arts. The point is, where there is false worship of false gods (or goddesses), there will be demonic activity in direct proportion.

I believe that we can trace the New Age Movement, as well as most cultish practices, to ancient pagan religions. We should also note that the Greeks acknowledged powers even higher than Zeus. They were called MOIRA (fate) and KER (doom). These two powers were in the control of DAIMONS (demons), the guardian spirits of the heavenlies.

I have also discovered a fascinating bit of information about how the early Romans named their deities. In certain instances, a mysterious voice came out of nowhere after a period of unrestrained zeal. The functions of these deities were to be sharply defined, and in approaching them it was essential to use their proper names and titles. If one knew the deity's name, one would be assured of a hearing.

I believe that these ancient demons who once ruled the skies over Ephesus, Corinth, Athens and other ancient powerful cities, receiving worship through graven images, idols, statues, and so on, are now ruling the skies over the modern world cities of importance, such as New York, Chicago, Los Angeles, San Francisco, Tokyo, Moscow, and even your city.

In Isaiah 14:12-20, the Bible describes the fall of Lucifer. Please note verse 17, which says, "Who made the world as a wilderness and destroyed its cities ... ?" Verse 21 continues, "Prepare slaughter for his children, because of the iniquity of their fathers, lest they rise up and possess the land, and fill the face of the world with cities [their kind]."

It is Satan's plan to destroy the cities! How? First, by eradicating all forms of worship of God. Second, by raising up some form of pagan worship to replace it. Satan understands man's basic need to worship and he takes full advantage of that for his own warped purposes.

When Satan and his minions have established a foothold, the spirit of Babylon can undermine a city, country, or even an empire until it has been totally destroyed.

Revelation 17 speaks of the "Mystery, Babylon the Great, The Mother of Harlots and of the Abominations of the Earth." In verse 15 it speaks of her influence over nations, peoples and tongues. She has historically corrupted every empire with her sorceries. Could this harlot be the infamous Semiramis, the mother of idolatry?

Storming Hell's Brazen Gates

6

Blow the Trumpet, Sound the Alarm

Christians, the war is on!

The Apostle Paul wrote, "For we do not wrestle against flesh and blood, but against principalities, against powers, against the rulers of the darkness of this age, against spiritual hosts of wickedness in the heavenly places" (Ephesians 6:12). We may not be wrestling with flesh and blood, but we are most certainly wrestling! During my sophomore year in high school I was very active in the sport of wrestling. I discovered soon enough that when the whistle blows, one of two things happens. You either have a hold of your opponent, or your opponent has a hold of you!

This truism certainly has validity in our spiritual warfare with the devil!

To Take Our Cities, We Should:

1. Proclaim a fast with prayer.

2. Identify the principality over the city.

3. Determine its geographical location.

4. Call him/her by name. We know our chief adversary by name and title; some of them are Satan, Belial, Devil, Prince, Dragon, Serpent, Adversary, Accuser, Wicked One, Enemy, Tempter, and Thief.

After old Lucifer was cast out of heaven, the Lord saw to it that we could identify the "god of this world" by his name and deeds. There are other principalities which are also named, e.g. Beelzebub and Legion. Beelzebub, the Prince of Devils, was worshiped by the ancient Philistines (2 Kings 1:2). He was then called Baalzebub, the Lord of the Flies. He was a most vile and contemptible idol. Demons on earth prefer to possess flesh and blood, especially human, but if necessary they will inhabit animals, as described in Mark 5:9. Legion, being comprised of some 6,000 demons, begged Christ not to cast them into the Abyss, but to allow them to enter the swine. Demons will also frequently possess idols and images of wood and stone during times of worship and oblation.

A minister friend was telling me of how, when he was in a certain area of Asia - Tibet, I believe - he was being shown a huge statue of Buddha. As the guide took him to the back of the idol he pointed to a hole and commented, "Here's where the spirits enter at the time of worship."

Remember, Satan craves worship, and he'll take it any way he can get it. He'll use a statue of Buddha, a totem pole, a golden calf, he isn't choosy. There is also a ruler of the demons who is presently incarcerated in the bottomless pit. The king's name is Abaddon in the Hebrew tongue and, interestingly, Apollyon in the Greek. In Revelation 9:11 we read: "And they had as king over them the angel of the bottomless pit, whose name in Hebrew is Abaddon, but in Greek he has the name Apollyon."

Apollyon comes from the name Apollo, who, according to myth, was the son of Zeus - remember, we previously discussed Athena (Minerva). He was called a pastoral and musician god and was also a god of prophecy and destruction. In some cases, but not all, when dealing with common demons we must first identify them. For example, Jesus asked for a demon's identity.

In Mark 5:9 Jesus asked, "What is your name?" and the demon answered, "My name [it was the leader speaking] is Legion, for we are many." Though we cannot be sure why in this instance Jesus demanded identity, we do know that He always followed His Father's will and was totally Holy Spirit-led.

I cannot be too emphatic. When we deal with the princes and rulers of the heavenlies, they must be identified!

Even the ancient Greeks knew how to approach their gods (whom we now identify as "principalities"). They were always approached by name and title. I am convinced that through prayer and fasting, the Spirit of God will show us who and where these present rulers are. Only then will we be able to focus our militant prayers like a rifle (as opposed to our present buckshot approach), taking keen aim at our adversary and allowing God to work through us to bring down those gates of brass.

Commitment: The Essence of Victory

Serious city-takers take serious measures; for instance, proclaiming a fast with fervent prayer. A personal confession: I am not into fasting. I have no great propensity toward lengthy prayers. But with sacrifice and obedience comes victory and blessing! I suppose that if these things came naturally we'd all be doing more of them.

Recently I heard a great teaching on Isaiah 58 by Jack Hayford. The first five verses are a rebuke against the "religious" fasters. Is it really necessary?

Some folks fast just to lose weight, to get noticed, to force God's hand, to appear pious or with other wrong motives - the Lord takes a dim view of that kind of fast. In fact, in verses 3 through 5, we read, " ...'Why have we afflicted our souls, and You take no notice?' In fact, in the day of your fast you find pleasure, and exploit all your laborers. Indeed you fast for strife and debate, and to strike with the fist of wickedness. You will not fast as you do this day, to make your voice heard on high. Is it a fast that I have chosen, a day for a man to afflict his soul? Is it to bow down his head like a bulrush, and to spread out sackcloth and ashes? Would you call this a fast, and an acceptable day to the Lord?"

Vain religious exercise is really not what moves the hand of God, even though His patience is unlimited; but He goes on to say that a godly fast is one with proper priorities:

1. To loose the bonds of wickedness.

2. To let the oppressed go free.

3. To break every yoke.

4. To become more benevolent and giving.

5. To speed up the healing process.

6. To gain protection (rear guard).

7. To receive answers to our petitions.

Then, the Lord says in verse 12, "Those from among you shall build the old waste places; You shall raise up the foundations of many generations; And you shall be called the Repairer of the Breach, the Restorer of Streets to Dwell In."

Not a bad legacy to leave if the Lord tarries, is it? To be called a "restorer, a repairer, sounds very good to me!

We read throughout the Scriptures that in desperate times God's leaders would proclaim a fast to seek the face of God. In Second Chronicles 20:1-3, "It happened after this that the people of Moab with the people of Ammon, and others with them besides the Ammonites, came to battle against Jehoshaphat. Then some came and told Jehoshaphat, saying, 'A great multitude is coming against you from beyond the sea, from Syria; and they are in Hazazon Tamar' (which is in En Gedi). And Jehoshaphat feared, and set himself to seek the Lord, and proclaimed a fast throughout all Judah."

Our biggest challenge is to get pastors and church leaders to SEE the enemy's forces!

Recently I had lunch with several ministers from well-known denominations. We were discussing spiritual warfare here in the Bay Area and they said, "Dick, our biggest problem is convincing our leaders and congregations that there really are demons, and that they are here in our own backyard!"

Here in America?

Some people at least acknowledge the existence of evil spirits, but they believe that they are all in India, Africa, Haiti, or some distant land - but not in the good old U.S. of A.

They must think that our immigration officials stop them at the borders if they don't have a visa or green card. But I tell you just as wolves will come in sheep's clothing, demons will adapt to whatever society they invade, and they invade every level of society in every land.

We are told in the Scriptures that demons can assume the appearance of frogs (Revelation 16:13) or locusts (Revelation 9:3); others have seen them as monkey-like or even ape-like creatures. One wonders if the so-called cavemen whose images we've discovered, or even the bones which date back millenniums or even millions of years, aren't really the bodies of what we today call demons.

To me it is obvious that the lower-ranking demons are disembodied spirits who crave houses of flesh and blood, human or animal. Angels don't ordinarily need a body to function. They are spirit beings. In contrast, the demons need bodies to operate on earth. The ruling class, called principalities and powers, are certainly Satan's angels. They are those who aligned themselves with him at the time of the fall. But there is another category of fallen, outcast angels held in a region called Tartarus. It is mentioned in Second Peter 2:4. "For if God did not spare the angels who sinned, but cast them down to hell and delivered them into chains of darkness, to be reserved for judgment..."

Sons of God

Some teach that this group of angels, called "sons of God," were the ones who fornicated with the daughters of men, and that the resultant creatures were the giants described in Genesis 6:1-4. "Now it came to pass, when men began to multiply on the face of the earth, and daughters were born to them, that the sons of God saw the daughters of men, that they were beautiful; and they took wives for themselves of all whom they chose. And the Lord said, 'My Spirit shall not strive with man forever, for he is indeed flesh; yet his days shall be one hundred and twenty years.' There were giants on earth in those days, and also afterward, when the sons of God came in to the daughters of men and they bore children to them. Those were the mighty men who were of old, men of renown." As Jude says, in verses 6-7, "And the angels who did not keep their proper domain, but left their own habitation, He has reserved in everlasting chains under darkness for the judgment of the great day; as Sodom and Gomorrah, and the cities around them in a similar manner to these, having given themselves over to sexual immorality and gone after strange flesh, are set forth as an example, suffering the vengeance of eternal fire."

Scholars have been going around and around over this issue for years, yet it is evident that Satan has his angels. Another group is bound in Tartarus (a lower region of hell), and evil spirits are roaming the earth looking for dwelling places so that they can take up residence and bring misery. The actions of this invisible host are being orchestrated by the Master of Evil.

If you wish more information on the disembodied spirits and their activities, *see Dake's Annotated Reference Bible* under the section on demons and devils (page 32, Cyclopedic Index).

Identifying the Principality over Your City

Through prayer and fasting, the Holy Spirit will reveal the kind of principality over your community.

One of the best ways to identify the spirit over your area is to go to your local library and research your town or city's beginnings. Who were the influential pioneers? What kind of people were they?

If possible, find their religious backgrounds. A friend from South Africa told me about a revival which broke out around a particular neighborhood. Because of this area's heritage, one deeply rooted in witchcraft and the occult, and because this was still being practiced, the Word of the Lord was not being received. People have told me that the seeds of witchcraft in upper New England are still alive and preventing revival from coming to that beautiful section of our land.

Pleading the Blood

The people of God need to learn how to break curses over their cities, states, and even whole nations. Jesus has given us plenty of fire-power. Convincing the Church of the availability of this power is our greatest challenge!

Unfortunately, many sweet brothers and sisters seem too content just being the Lord's little lambs, when our Captain is calling His followers to be SOLDIERS.

A smart pastor will gently but firmly shepherd his flock through a "renewing of the mind" process. One of the worst things we as leaders can do is to push unprepared sheep to the front line of battle! Even our nation's military branches understand the absolute necessity of boot camp.

Before we teach "authority" and "power," we must first teach commitment, faithfulness, attitude, accountability, submission, and even tithing.

I've met scores of folks who come through my office boasting of their calling to the front lines of ministry. "Pastor Dick, I'm on the cutting edge of this move of God. I have a word for you and this church." "Oh, really! Where do you attend church?" "I go to several churches as the Lord leads." "Well, friend," I ask, "Which one do you tithe to?" "Tithe? That's under the law, Pastor. We've been redeemed from the law!" "Then who are you submitted to?" "My covering is the Father, Son, and Holy Ghost!"

No Time to Play Around

Sad, sad, indeed! Little boys and girls playing at something as important as Church! Needless to say, these very misguided souls spend their whole lives bouncing from church to church looking for a platform from which to share their "vision."

On the way to church a few years ago my then eleven-year-old daughter, Sarah, said: "Dad, I want a Porsche - a red one!" I replied, "Well, honey, first you have to be sixteen to drive a car, and even before that you'll have to learn how. Secondly, you'll need a great-paying job to be able to afford the car, insurance and upkeep."

A frown slowly crept over her face and she slumped back into her seat. She had shared her desire and I gave her responsibility! Just then my seven-year-old son, Jesse, blurted, "Daddy, I want a Lamborghini - and I want you to pay for it!"

I must confess that my kids are a lot like some church people I know. They want the blessings without the effort - or worse yet, they want you to do all the work for them.

In teaching "warfare" we have to be careful that people don't get into some sort of witch-hunt. What I mean is that we must make sure that the goals are clearly defined. If they are not, people will be casting demons out of door-knobs, neckties, coffee pots, whatever. A wise teacher will lead his students away from the lunatic fringe.

Locating the Powers of Darkness

This is a fairly new concept, but I believe an essential one. In our cities (yours and mine) there are hotbeds of demonic activity. At a recent conference at Church on the Way, Jack Hayford told how the Lord has revealed the exact location of the principality over his area there in Southern California. That evening as I returned to my hotel room I began to plead with God to show me where San Jose's stronghold was. Immediately the answer came, and I wasn't really surprised. Discretion dictates that I not publicly reveal the location or name the source. However, I will tell you that it's a powerful and influential place.

Since then we've discovered another hot spot of demon activity in our city.

Without my revealing this spiritual revelation to anyone except my wife Carla, calls began to come in concerning these particular locations.

The Word's Out

News about Jubilee's declaration of war on the "heavenlies" soon spread throughout the community. I received several confirmations that we were on the right track, and other churches (not all of them charismatic) have joined ranks as we begin warfare on Satan's stranglehold on our city.

In the meantime, I called a special meeting of seasoned veterans of prayer to discuss privately how we can purge the skies over these two locations. Nearly 900 prayer warriors showed up on an off night and we formed teams to surround those places mentioned, in addition to other strategic areas throughout the valley.

At midnight preceding Easter Sunday we took certain vantage points which gave us a good view of the whole Bay Area. We ascended mountaintops, we took rooms on the top levels of certain hotels. Some got permission to go to the rooftops of the higher buildings and office complexes. At the appointed hour we broke the seals from a proclamation which had been prepared previously.

This proclamation was a decree to the dark powers over San Jose and the surrounding communities that we were taking back our land in Jesus' Name.

In the Bible, kings issued written decrees. According to definition, a decree is an official order, law, or proclamation. When God's kings and priests (you and I, according to Revelation 1:6) take our rightful places of authority and learn how to issue decrees, the squatters of the heavenlies will certainly be deposed. We read in Job 22:27-28, "Thou shalt make thy prayer unto him, and he shall hear thee, and thou shalt... also decree a thing, and it shall be established unto thee: and the light shall shine upon thy ways" (KJV).

For the light of the Gospel to flood our cities, we must issue a royal decree to the principalities and powers, the ones who barricade the heavens. They will have no choice but to move on. It is then that the skies of brass will open for us and turn golden and glorious!

Knocking down the high places before taking the land is a biblical principle. In Judges chapter 6, God chose to use a young man named Gideon to free Israel from the Midianites. Because of open idolatry, Israel had provoked the Lord to remove His protective hand. The incident is fairly humorous. In verse one we discover Gideon cowering in the winepress, threshing a little wheat, and hiding from the Midianites.

The Angel of the Lord appears to him and says, "The Lord is with you, you mighty man of valor." "Who, me?" an exasperated Gideon responds. "With me? If God is with me, then why has all this happened to us? Where are the miracles our fathers told us about? You know, the Red Sea and all that?" Gideon didn't realize that miracles come to a holy people, and Israel had gone whoring after other gods. Even Gideon's own father had erected an altar to Baal as well as a wooden image of Asherah.

That night the Lord told him to destroy the altar and cut down the wooden image. In its place God instructed him to build an altar "to your God and confirm the covenant with blood."

A burnt offering was made only after the high places were torn down ... it was then that deliverance came.

Let's not get excited about building new altars until we tear down some old demonic ones. As you and I, Gideon didn't look too much like a warrior; but he didn't have to.

The Lord said, "Don't worry, I'll do the fighting for you, just be obedient to Me."

Second Chronicles 34:2-4 tells of the young reformer Josiah. In verse 2, we read, "And he did what was right in the sight of the Lord, and walked in the ways of his father David; he did not turn aside to the right hand or to the left."

In the eighth year of his reign, while he was still young, he began to seek the God of his father, David; and in the twelfth year he began to purge Judah and Jerusalem of the high places, the wooden images, the carved images and the molded images.

They broke down the altars of Baal in his presence. The incense altars which were above them he cut down; and the wooden images, the carved images, he broke in pieces and then he made dust of them and scattered them on the graves of those who had sacrificed to them.

A local pastor and friend, Rich Marshall, has been traveling back and forth to Argentina to get an eyewitness account of the revival which is breaking out there. He suggested that I contact an evangelist, Ed Silvoso, who could give me a report of the warfare being waged against the evil forces of that nation. Rev. Silvoso told me of an incident in the town of Adrogue.

Many groups had tried unsuccessfully to establish a church in that town. The lone survivor was a Baptist congregation pastored by a Brother Lorenzo. The believers of that town located the trouble spot, a house occupied by a demonized woman. This person was involved in all kinds of satanic worship.

They led this woman to the Lord after a deliverance, and a powerful move of God ensued. The last word that

Brother Silvoso got was that the principality was not giving up easily, but that progress was being made on all fronts.

Another stirring account comes from the area called Arroyo Seco (Dry Creek) in Argentina. Here a strong warlock (male witch) had a stranglehold over a large area encompassing 109 towns and villages. In all these places there was not a single evangelical church - not one! Two and a half years ago the believers broke the curse on their land and today 82 of the 109 communities have growing churches.

In a sense, I believe, we are deceived into thinking that ours is a "Christian" nation. Our forefathers certainly intended it to be! It is also true that millions of Americans who "hold fast the profession of their faith" are "Christian Americans;" but it is ludicrous to claim that we are a righteous nation when so many of the laws of the land are unscriptural!

America, What Have We Done?

We pride ourselves as the "land of the free, the home of the brave," but we forgot to define "freedom." Our so-called freedom has become a snare. Like the Jews after King David, we have gone whoring after other gods! Hindu and Buddhist temples are springing up as quickly as, if not more rapidly than, Christian churches in the state of California.

As the backslidden Hebrews erected altars to Baal and Ashtoreth on land dedicated to Jehovah God, so we have broken the vow made by our fathers to honor the one true God.

Apparently God knew just how severe the temptation was, for He began the Ten Commandments by saying, "I am the Lord your God, who brought you out of the land of

Egypt, out of the house of bondage. You shall have no other gods before Me. You shall not make for yourself any carved image, or any likeness of anything that is in heaven above, or that is in the earth beneath, or that is in the water under the earth; you shall not bow down to them nor serve them. For I, the Lord your God, am a jealous God, visiting the iniquity of the fathers on the children to the third and fourth generations of those who hate Me, but showing mercy to thousands, to those who love Me and keep My commandments" (Exodus 20:2-6).

7

The Gates of Brass

"... the kingdom of heaven suffers violence, and the violent take it by force" (Matthew 11: 12). I say, "Oh God, let a Holy Ghost spirit of violence take over Your people."

Some of the most encouraging Scriptures for the Church corporately are found in Matthew 16:17-19. Following Peter's excited confession, "You are the Christ, the Son of the living God," Jesus proceeds to say, "Upon this rock [revelation] I will build my church, and the gates of Hades [hell] shall not prevail against it."

What is Jesus saying here? Once a person perceives the true identity of Jesus through Holy Spirit revelation, and, as importantly, who we are in Christ, no hellish evil powers can keep us from our God and His blessings.

What is a gate? It is a structure that can be swung, drawn, or lowered to block an entrance or passageway. "An opening in a wall or fence for entrance and exit" (*American Heritage Dictionary,* page 549).

Hell's Domain

Hell, according to the Bible, is a literal place or region for incarcerating souls, both human and angelic. Hell is also described as a condition. In James 3:6, hell is pictured as a source of the evil done by the misuse of the tongue.

The dictionary also describes hell as "the abode of

evil spirits."

Certainly the prison house of the underworld is full of evil spirits, but I have another thought to suggest: The skies (heavenlies) above us are also the abode of Satan, the prince of the power of the air, and his spirit hosts. I do believe that Satan and his army have set up gates ... gates of brass ... over our cities. These gates are blocking God's blessing. They are also hindering God's angelic host from bringing help and answered prayers to our diseased and hurting world. Oh, I know a few of the faithful have broken through and received a measure of blessing; but more universally, the hellish skies are still intact and presided over by a satanic host.

Historically, the gates were the most significant area of a city. It was there that the elders and magistrates congregated. The powerful and the ones who held positions of authority sat at the gates. In Proverbs 31 , we read of the virtuous woman's husband, "He is known in the gates."

Lot, Abraham's nephew, sat at the gates of Sodom (Genesis 19). Civic, military, even major decisions of business and commerce were settled at the city's gates.

Dr. Lester Sumrall published a book which I recommend in connection with this study. It is called Destroying the Gates of Hell. "The stronger the city gate, the safer the city." It stands to reason that an invading army would first endeavor to storm the gates. That would be their focal point, for where else could their horses and machines of war gain an entrance? Usually, when the city's gates came down, the enemy conquered.

The Evil Skies

Above our cities today, here in America and all over the world, the evil elders, magistrates and rulers are sitting at the gates keeping mankind in submission and preventing the angelic hosts from assisting us in the manner that Hebrews 1:14 promises: "Are they not all ministering spirits sent forth to minister for those who will inherit salvation?" Occasionally a gate will be opened through focused prayer and intercession, as, for example, in Korea or in Argentina. But these are isolated instances.

Let me finish the quotation I started from Matthew 16:18-19, where Jesus promised "... and the gates of Hades shall not prevail [overpower, block, be strong] against it [My Church]. And I will give you [us] the keys of the kingdom of heaven, and whatever you bind on earth [through prayer] will be bound in heaven, and whatever you loose on earth will be loosed in heaven."

In ancient times keys were symbols of authority and power. The one who had the keys had the assured access. Later on, in Matthew 28:18-19, Jesus said, "All authority has been given to Me in heaven and on earth [that includes the "heavenlies" in between and the region beneath the earth]. Go therefore..."

Victory over Iniquity

"Go because I am authorizing you to take My place as kings and priests [Revelation 1:6] and loose men everywhere from Satan's control." Before we can loose mankind from hell's dominion, we must first pull down the strongholds.

As kings and priests, we have the titles and the Name to confront the principalities. They will be totally powerless to prevail against God's royal family. Not only will we open the gates, but we will demolish the gates of brass which have enshrouded our cities for many centuries.

Storming Hell's Brazen Gates

8

Claiming the Promises

A beautiful promise is found in Genesis 22:17: "In blessing I will bless you, and in multiplying I will multiply your descendants as the stars of the heaven and as the sand which is on the seashore; and your descendants shall possess the gate of their enemies." Here God is prophesying over Abraham and his seed (the Church, the true spiritual descendants of father Abraham). I say "glory to God" on that one!

In Isaiah 28:5-6, the Bible says, "In that day the Lord of hosts will be for a crown of glory and a diadem of beauty to the remnant of His people, for a spirit of justice to him who sits in judgment, and for strength to those who turn back the battle at the gate." Again, in Isaiah chapter 45, the Word of the Lord came with prophetic overtones to the twentieth-century Church; "Thus says the Lord to His anointed, to Cyrus whose right hand I have held - to subdue nations before him and loose the armor of kings, to open before him the double doors, so that the gates will not be shut: 'I will go before you and make the crooked places straight; I will break in pieces the gates of bronze [brass] and cut the bars of iron. I will give you the treasures of darkness and hidden riches of secret places, That you may know that I, the Lord, Who call you by your name, am the God of Israel' " (Isaiah 45:1-3).

We read in Isaiah 45, verse 8, "Rain down, you heavens, from above, and let the skies pour down righteousness; let the earth open, let them bring forth salvation, and let righteousness spring up together. I, the Lord, have created it."

What was it that the Lord said? First, He said we are to strip the enemy powers (kings and princes) of their armor. Then we should open the double doors (gates). The Lord promises, "I will go before you and smooth out the path, then I'll demolish the brass gates." It is then that He promises that we will reap the spoils. In this case "treasures" means people who are precious in His sight, people who are dwelling in darkness and oppression, aimlessly drifting through life.

In Exodus 19:5 the Lord said, "Now therefore, if you will indeed obey My voice and keep My covenant, then you shall be a special treasure to Me above all people; for all the earth is Mine." One of the ways the Lord destroyed the enemy was to bring confusion into their camp. A fascinating example of this is found once again in the story of King Jehoshaphat and the badly outnumbered troops of Israel.

An unholy alliance between the people of Ammon, Moab, and Mount Seir resulted in their combined armies coming to do battle with Jehoshaphat.

He cried to the Lord and proclaimed a fast. The Spirit of the Lord spoke through Jahaziel, a Levite and descendant of Asaph. The Word from the Lord was, "Listen, all you of Judah and you inhabitants of Jerusalem, and you, King Jehoshaphat! Thus says the Lord to you: 'Do not be afraid nor dismayed because of this great multitude, for the battle is not yours, but God's. Tomorrow go down against them. They will surely come up by the ascent of Ziz, and you will find them at the end of the brook before the Wilderness of Jeruel [God pinpoints the enemy's location for them]. You will not need to fight in this battle. Position yourselves, stand still and see the salvation of the Lord, who is with you, O Judah and Jerusalem!' " (2 Chronicles 20:14-17)

Verse 22 says that the Lord set up ambushes against the enemy. Confusion came upon the enemy and they began to destroy each other. Apparently there was no love between these warring "partners" to begin with.

As I mentioned previously, the evil hosts have no great love for one another. They only cooperate because they are ordered to by Satan.

I believe that through prayer God will vex our enemies similarly. If we follow His directions, they will turn on each other.

9

The Gathering

Now ... back to our plan of attack.

The task at hand is too big for one pastor or one church to assume. There must be a uniting of the candlesticks (churches) to launch a laser-ray assault on the brazen skies. If our heart's desire is to see a city coming to God, we must prove it by a consecrated leadership. That must be the number one priority: an attack led by leaders who are willing to be ordained (dedicated) to the task as never before. Sheep follow shepherds!

A united effort is absolutely essential. A proclaimed fast is an excellent starting point. Remember, we are told in Isaiah 58 that before we can loose the bonds of wickedness to let the oppressed go free and break every yoke, we must fast a fast that the Lord has chosen.

Corporate Effort

A fast must be coupled with much intercessory prayer. Congregations must keep the Christian Sabbath as holy unto the Lord. They must turn away their feet from doing their own pleasures on Sunday. Isaiah 58:13-14 instructs, "If you turn away your foot from the Sabbath, from doing your pleasure on My holy day, and call the Sabbath a delight, the holy day of the Lord honorable, and shall honor Him, not doing your own ways, nor finding your own pleasure, nor speaking your own words, then you shall delight yourself in the Lord; and I will cause you to ride on the high hills of the earth, and feed you with the heritage of Jacob your father. The mouth of the Lord has spoken."

Jesus said that there are certain demons (the strong kind) who are only cast out (brought down) through prayer and fasting. As Matthew 17:21 states, "However, this kind does not go out except by prayer and fasting."

It is fundamental that the pastors and leaders convince their congregations that it can be done - we can take back our cities! There is no substitute for faith and confidence. Just as in the natural it is suicidal to enter an arena of combat with a defeatist attitude, the same applies to the spiritual realm. The spoils go to the victors, not the timid "tryers." Once our hand is to the plow, there is no turning back.

Take Heed

Of this you can be sure: once war is corporately declared on the heavenlies, all hell is going to break loose. Satan's government will not easily be challenged. Scores of seasoned saints have privately asked me, "Does our church really understand what we're buying into?" And to this I can only reply, "It's too late now to turn back. I have already issued the challenge and sounded the alarm!"

Our Primary Focus

Paul wrote in his letter to the Ephesians, " ... to the intent that now the manifold wisdom of God might be made known by the church to the principalities and powers in heavenly places" (3:10).

Don't skip over this portion too fast! Paul prefaces verse 10 with, "And to make all people see what is the fellowship [stewardship] of the mystery, which from the beginning of the ages has been hidden in God who created all things through Jesus Christ; *to the intent...*" (v.9, emphasis added) This means that for this purpose, for this reason you and I (the Church) will tell the principalities and powers who is in control!

The Body of Christ is reclaiming that which the devil has stolen.

We must also be possessed with a spirit of patience. Our inaugural efforts are in the invisible realm. We cannot gauge success simply by how quickly our pews and coffers fill.

Visible growth is not always a true barometer of whether a city is coming to God. Yet I am convinced that the Lord will build His Church as long as our labors are not in vain.

Well, troops, thank God that the "weapons of our warfare are not carnal but mighty in God for pulling down strongholds" (2 Corinthians 10:4).

I earnestly admonish you, keep the full armor of God on! Don't take it off! Wear it to bed, take it to work, make sure that your sword is sharp! Be a battle-ready soldier! STAND! Take your place in destiny!

"I saw Satan fall like lightning from heaven" (Luke 10:18).

So be it! Amen!